Jackie Silberg

Brain Games

for babies, toddlers & twos

BARNES & NOBLE
BOOKS
NEW YORK

THE AUTHOR

Jackie Silberg is an acclaimed speaker, teacher and trainer on both early childhood development and music. She has published numerous books on games to play with your baby, toddler or child.

This edition first published in Great Britain in 2002 by Hamlyn, a division of Octopus Publishing Group Ltd, 2–4 Heron Quays, London E14 4JP

Distributed in the United States and Canada by Sterling Publishing Co., Inc., 387 Park Avenue South, New York, NY 10016–8810

Text copyright © Jackie Silberg 1999, 2000 Design, photographs and layout © Octopus Publishing Group Ltd 2002

ISBN 0-7607-6016-0

A CIP catalogue record for this book is available from the British Library

Printed and bound in China

10 9 8 7 6 5 4 3 2 1

contents

Introduction

Playing with babies and toddlers is delightful. Even very young babies enjoy being held, rocked, nuzzled and cuddled. This book is about helping to 'grow' the brain of these lovely human beings by playing meaningful games with them. Whether it's through singing, dancing, cuddling, rocking, talking, smelling or tasting, you can encourage the pathways of your child's brain to make new connections.

How the brain works

By the time a child is three, the brain has formed 1,000 trillion connections – about twice as many as adults have. Some brain cells, called neurons, have already been hard-wired to other cells before birth. They control the baby's heartbeat, breathing and reflexes, and regulate other functions essential to survival. The rest of the brain connections are waiting to be 'hooked up'.

The connections neurons make with each other are called synapses. While various parts of the brain develop at different rates, study after study has shown that the peak production period for synapses is from birth to about the age of ten. During that time, the receptive branches of the nerve cells, called dendrites, are growing and reaching out to form trillions upon trillions of synapses. One cell can be connected to 10,000 other cells. The brain's weight triples to nearly adult size. Periods of rapid synapse production in specific parts of the brain seem to correspond to the development of behaviours linked to those parts of the brain. Scientists believe the stimulation that babies and young children receive determines which synapses form in the brain – that is, which pathways become hard-wired.

How does the brain know which connections to keep? This is where early experience comes into play. Through repetition, brain connections become permanent. Conversely, a connection that is not used at all or often enough is unlikely to survive. For example, a child who is rarely spoken to or read to in the early years may have difficulty mastering language skills later on. A child who is rarely played with may have difficulty with social adjustment in later life. An infant's brain thrives on feedback from its environment. It wires itself into a thinking and emotional organ from the things it experiences. The circuits that form in the brain influence the development of a child. So a child immersed in language from birth is likely to learn to speak very well. A baby whose coos are met with smiles, rather than apathy, is likely to become emotionally responsive.

New research findings

Scientists have learned more in the past ten years about how the human brain works than in all of previous history. Their discovery that early childhood experiences profoundly shape the infant brain is changing the way we think about the needs of children.

Recent brain research has produced three key findings. First, an individual's capacity to learn and thrive in a variety of settings depends on the interplay between nature (genetic endowment) and nurture (the kind of care, stimulation and teaching received). Second, the human brain is uniquely constructed to benefit from experience and from good teaching during the first years of life. And third, while the opportunities and risks are greatest during the first years of life, learning takes place throughout the human life cycle.

The very best way to develop a baby's brain connections is to supply what babies need, starting with attentive parents and carers. Babies and toddlers flourish in an environment that is interesting to explore, that is safe and that is filled with people who respond to their emotional and intellectual requirements – people who will sing to them, hug them, talk to them and read to them. All these brain connections are not meant to push early learning but rather to develop the potential for future learning. When brain development happens as it should, future learning is likely to be successful. The games in this book develop the brain capacity of babies, toddlers and two-year-olds. They are the building blocks of future learning – a good, solid beginning for little ones. And they are fun too!

Birth to 3 months

Snuggle, buggle, I love you

WHAT RESEARCH SAYS

Research shows that the more an infant is cuddled, snuggled and held, the more secure and independent she will be when she is older.

This game develops bonding between you and your baby.

❀ Hold your baby in your arms and rock her back and forth.

❀ As you rock, say the words, 'Snuggle, buggle, I love you.'

❀ On the word 'you', kiss a part of her body – head, nose, toes.

❀ As your child grows older, she may ask to play this game.

Baby talk

WHAT RESEARCH SAYS

Babies respond to 'parentese' – the high-pitched sounds adults make when talking to babies.

When you speak 'parentese' to infants, you are communicating with them and encouraging vocal responses. This in turn develops language skills.

❀ Say things like, 'You're such a sweet baby' or 'Look at those ten little toes.'

❀ As you speak in 'parentese', hold the baby near to your face and look directly into her eyes.

Soothing music

WHAT RESEARCH SAYS

Newborns possess a natural response to music through their conditioning in the womb to rhythm, sound and movement.

Even small babies may be soothed by familiar music.

✿ Place a small cassette player near your baby.

✿ Choose soft instrumental music or lullabies to play.

✿ Music that has a repeated melody is very soothing to an infant because it is the kind of sound she heard in the womb.

✿ You could tape your dishwasher or washing machine and play this to your baby too, because these are also similar to the sounds of the womb.

Hugs and kisses

WHAT RESEARCH SAYS

A child's capacity to control
emotions hinges on early
experiences and attachments.

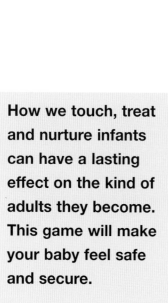

**How we touch, treat
and nurture infants
can have a lasting
effect on the kind of
adults they become.
This game will make
your baby feel safe
and secure.**

✿ Chant the following song as you rock and
   kiss your baby:
   'Hugs and kisses, I love you,
   I love you, I love you.
   Hugs and kisses, I love you.
   You're my baby.'

✿ When you are changing your baby's nappy,
   you can sing this song and kiss his nose, his
   toes, his fingers.

Where did it go?

WHAT RESEARCH SAYS

Neurons for vision begin forming during the first few months of life. Activities that stimulate a baby's sight will ensure good visual development.

Play this game often because it will help your baby's brain capacity to grow.

✿ Hold a brightly coloured object in front of your baby.

✿ Slowly move it around and talk about how bright it is.

✿ When you are sure that your baby is looking at the object, slowly move it to one side.

✿ Keep moving it back and forth to encourage him to follow it with his eyes.

Note: As with any game, watch for signs that your baby is tired of the game and ready to rest or play something different.

The rattle game

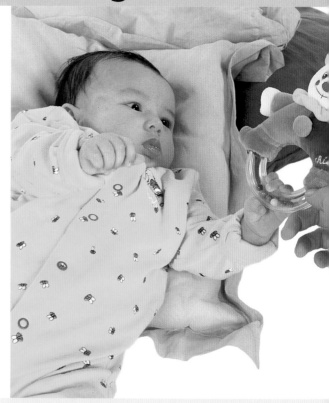

WHAT RESEARCH SAYS

An infant's brain thrives on feedback from its environment and 'wires' itself into a thinking and emotional organ based on early experiences.

The combination of sight and sound will encourage your baby to make connections.

✿ Hold a rattle in front of your baby and shake it gently.

✿ As you shake the rattle, sing any song or the following to the tune of 'Old MacDonald':
> 'Rattle, rattle, shake, shake, shake, E-I-E-I-O,
> Rattle, rattle, shake, shake, shake, E-I-E-I-O.'

✿ When you are sure that your baby is watching the rattle, slowly move it to one side and sing the song again.

✿ Continue moving the rattle to different places in the room and watch as your baby moves his head in the direction of the sound.

✿ Put the rattle in your baby's hand and sing the song again.

✿ Babies love singing and later, when they are ready to talk, they will try to imitate sounds they've heard.

Follow the action

WHAT RESEARCH SAYS

By two months babies can distinguish features on a face.

Babies love to look at faces, especially the faces of people they love.

✿ Try different facial expressions and sounds to develop your baby's vision and hearing.

✿ Here are some ideas:
  • Sing a song using big lip movements.
  • Blink your eyes.
  • Stick out your tongue.
  • Make contortions with your mouth.
  • Make lip sounds.
  • Cough or yawn.

Here's my finger

WHAT RESEARCH SAYS

Just reaching for an object
helps the brain to develop
hand–eye coordination.

**This game will
strengthen a baby's
hands and fingers,
while developing
tracking skills.**

- ❀ Hold your baby in your lap or lie her on her back.

- ❀ Put your index finger in her hand.

- ❀ She will probably grasp your finger, as this is a natural reflex with newborns.

- ❀ Each time she grasps your finger, say positive words like, 'That's my wonderful girl!' or 'You're so strong!'

Sensory experiences

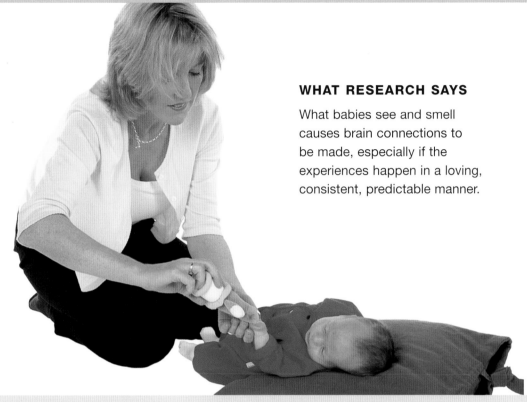

WHAT RESEARCH SAYS

What babies see and smell causes brain connections to be made, especially if the experiences happen in a loving, consistent, predictable manner.

Exposing your baby to many different sensations will broaden his awareness of himself and the world.

✿ Try rubbing your baby's arms with different fabrics. Satin, wool and towelling are good examples to start with.

✿ Give your baby an opportunity to experience different smells. Go outside and smell a flower, or try a freshly cut orange.

Note: Be careful not to overstimulate your baby. Watch for signs that he is tired of the game.

Bend those knees

WHAT RESEARCH SAYS

Strengthening your baby's thigh muscles is important for future crawling and walking.

As long as you do this exercise gently you won't cause your baby any discomfort and he will enjoy it.

✿ Place your baby on his back and carefully pull both legs until they are straight.

✿ When his legs are straight, lightly tap the bottoms of his feet.

✿ He will point his toes downward and bend his knees.

✿ As you do this game, sing the following to the tune of 'Ring-a-ring o' Roses':
'Bending, bending, bending,
Little knees are bending,
Bending, bending,
Hip hooray!'

✿ End a rhyme with some kind of a cheer. Your baby will learn to anticipate it, and it makes the game more exciting.

Shadows

WHAT RESEARCH SAYS

The neurons for vision begin to form around two months. Stimulating a baby's sight will help make the visual connections.

Infants wake up many times during the night so it's good to have things to lull them gently back to sleep.

✿ Shadows cast on the wall by a night-light make interesting shapes and forms for your baby to look at.

✿ If you can arrange a mobile so that it reflects shadows, you will be helping to develop your baby's visual growth.

✿ When your child gets a little older, make shadow designs with your hands.

Hello

WHAT RESEARCH SAYS

At birth your baby can see best between 20 and 30 cm (8 and 12 inches) from his eyes.

When your baby sees your face, he will be content.

✿ Say the following poem with your face close to your baby's face:
  'Hello, hello, I love you very much.
  Hello, hello, my fingers they can touch.
  Hello, hello, I'll touch your little nose.
  (Touch baby's nose.)
  Hello, hello, I'll kiss your little nose.
  (Kiss baby's nose.)'

✿ Repeat this poem and change the last two lines to different parts of his face – ears, eyes, cheek, lips.

Non-verbal games

WHAT RESEARCH SAYS

Touching, holding and cuddling a baby not only comforts her, but helps her brain grow.

Holding your baby close to you will develop the secure attachment that she needs for her growth.

❀ Communicate with infants by looking into their eyes, holding them close to your body and responding to their sounds.

❀ Hold your baby close and walk around the room.

❀ Stop walking and look into her eyes, smile and rub noses.

❀ Start walking again, then stop. Repeat this several times.

Switching pitches

WHAT RESEARCH SAYS

When babies are in the womb, they are able to distinguish the sound of human voices.

According to brain researchers, when a baby hears a high-pitched voice (like 'parentese'), his heart rate increases, indicating that he feels secure and cheerful.

When you speak in a lower-pitched voice, your baby feels soothed and content.

✿ Try singing a song in a high voice and then repeat the same song in a low voice. Watch the reaction of your baby to the two different sounds.

Nappy-changing game

WHAT RESEARCH SAYS

Scientists are just now realizing how experiences after birth determine the actual 'wiring' of the human brain.

The changing mat is always a good place for developing motor skills.

✿ Why not give your baby interesting things to look at while she is being changed?

✿ Try hanging an inflatable ball from the ceiling close enough for you to touch, but out of your baby's reach.

✿ Make the ball move slowly while you are changing the nappy.

✿ Your baby will be fascinated by this and, before long, will try to reach out and touch the ball.

✿ When the nappy is changed, hold your baby and let her touch the ball.

✿ You could also hang a mobile with family pictures from the ceiling.

3 to 6 months

Look what I see

WHAT RESEARCH SAYS

Exercising visual skills is essential during the first six months of life.

Babies love to stare at interesting faces and colourful toys.

✿ Take several colourful toys and, one at a time, slowly move them back and forth in front of your baby to stimulate her vision.

✿ This is also the time when babies discover their hands. They watch and watch and learn that they can make them appear and disappear.

✿ Take your baby's hands and gently clap them in front of her face. As you do this, say the following poem:
   'Clap, clap, clap your hands,
   Clap your hands together.
   Put your hands on Mummy's face.
   (*Substitute name of the person doing the rhyme with baby.*)
   Clap your hands together.'

Nuggle nose

WHAT RESEARCH SAYS

Gently touching your baby will make him feel secure and safe, enabling him to become confident and, eventually, independent.

This game will help your baby form a close emotional bond with you.

✿ Hold your baby in the air and say, 'Nose, nose, nuggle nose.'

✿ On the word 'nuggle', bring him down and touch your nose to his.

✿ Keep repeating this game, touching noses on the word 'nuggle'.

✿ After you have played this a few times, say the word 'nuggle' more than once, always touching noses.

✿ For example, say, 'Nuggle, nuggle, nuggle, nose' and touch noses three times.

Going up the escalator

WHAT RESEARCH SAYS

Loving attachments help babies develop trust.

As well as building trust between you and your baby, this game will strengthen her muscles.

❀ Hold on to your baby's fingers and gently lift her arms as you say the following rhyme:
    'Going up the escalator,
    Up, up, up.
    Going down the escalator,
    Down, down, down.'

❀ Lift your baby's legs and say the rhyme.

❀ Continue lifting different parts of her body, saying the rhyme each time.

❀ Try ending with lifting her up in the air and down.

❀ Always give a kiss on the down part.

Choo choo train

WHAT RESEARCH SAYS

Dramatic speech encourages emotional expression in babies. This in turn activates the brain to release chemicals that help memory.

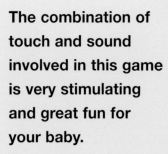

The combination of touch and sound involved in this game is very stimulating and great fun for your baby.

❀ As you say the following rhyme, move your fingers up your baby's arm and back down again:
   'Choo choo train, choo choo train,
   Going up the track.
   Toot, toot, toot, toot,
   Now it's coming back.'

❀ Repeat with the other arm.

❀ Be dramatic with the word 'toot' and soon your baby will be trying to make that sound.

Connect with conversation

WHAT RESEARCH SAYS

The number of words babies hear each day influences their future intelligence, social skills and scholastic achievements.

When you let your baby know that you are listening to him and that you like what he says, you are developing his language skills and confidence.

❁ Start a conversation with your baby. Say a short sentence like, 'It is a beautiful day today.'

❁ When your baby responds, mimic the sounds that he makes. Those simple sounds will later turn into words. As he talks, respond with a nod of your head or a smile.

❁ This indicates to your baby that you are listening to him and enjoying his sounds.

❁ Continue with another sentence. Always stop and listen to your baby's response.

Taping sounds

WHAT RESEARCH SAYS

Babies just four days old can distinguish one language from another and soon pay attention to the sounds (words) that matter.

This kind of stimulating environment assures good language skills for the future.

✿ Tape-record your baby's babbling.

✿ Play the sounds of the tape and see how she responds.

✿ Do the sounds get your baby excited? Does she talk back to the tape recorder?

✿ If your baby enjoys listening to the taped sounds, try other ones, like nature sounds.

Let's kick

WHAT RESEARCH SAYS

Repeating motor skills over and over strengthens the neural circuits that go from the brain's thinking areas to the motor areas and out to the nerves that move muscles.

Kicking develops motor skills and is something that babies love to do.

❀ Attach colourful items to your baby's ankles and watch him kick with glee.

❀ Many booties have brightly coloured toes that babies love to watch as they kick.

❀ Dangle a rattle or bells in front of his feet. Show him how to kick the rattle or bells.

Dance a baby

WHAT RESEARCH SAYS

Connecting rhythm, movement and bonding produces lots of brain 'wiring' that is likely to help babies in their future development.

This is a variation of an old English rhyme called 'Dance a Baby Diddy'.

❀ Hold your baby firmly under her arms and dance her on a soft surface.

❀ Say the rhyme and do the actions.
'Dance a baby diddy,
What can I do widdy?
Sit on a lap
(put baby on your lap),
And give her a pat
(gently pat her cheek),
Dance a baby diddy, dance a baby diddy
(go back to dancing).'

Wiggles and shuffles

WHAT RESEARCH SAYS

Wiggles and shuffles help the formation of the brain synapses that develop future large motor skills.

Babies wiggle themselves all over the place. These wiggles and shuffles are preparing them to crawl.

✿ Place your baby on his tummy and lie on the floor facing him.

✿ Put an interesting toy in front of him but just out of his reach.

✿ Move the toy (balls with jingles are good) back and forth.

✿ As he attempts to get the ball, he will probably shuffle forward a little.

✿ Give him a chance to retrieve the ball and praise him generously.

This kind of success develops great self-confidence.

Changing hands

WHAT RESEARCH SAYS

Repeating a motor skill over and over will develop neural circuits that move from the brain's thinking areas into the motor cortex and out to the nerves that move the muscles.

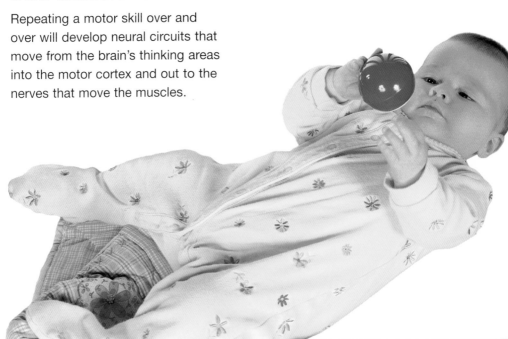

You can help strengthen the neural circuits in the brain by helping your baby practise changing hands. This game develops small motor skills and hand–eye coordination.

Between the ages of three and six months, your baby may begin to transfer an object from one hand to the other.

❀ Put a small rattle into one of her hands.

❀ Shake her hand with the rattle.

❀ Show her how to transfer the rattle to her other hand. These are the steps:
  • Put her empty hand on the rattle and she will automatically grab it.
  • Undo her fingers on the first hand, then kiss her fingers.

Hup, two, three, four

WHAT RESEARCH SAYS

Singing and dancing with your baby are two of the best things you can do to help 'wire' his brain.

Babies enjoy music and rhythm. When they were in the womb, they felt the rhythm of the heart and heard the sounds of the blood moving through the body.

❀ Hold your baby close to your body and move around the room as you sing your favourite songs. Any song will do as long as it's one that you like.

❀ Your baby will sense your joy and this will make him happy too.

❀ Try a marching cadence and say the words 'hup, two, three, four' as you march around the room.

❀ You can also sway, turn, tiptoe and take large, sweeping steps.

Roll Olympics

WHAT RESEARCH SAYS

Using their chest and arm muscles repeatedly gives babies the strength and elasticity for rolling over.

Helping your baby roll over from her tummy to her back will develop these muscles.

This is a fun game to play while encouraging your baby to roll over.

✿ Put your baby on her tummy on a soft and flat surface. Carpeted floors and the middle of beds are good for this game.

✿ Hold up a teddy bear in front of her face and do antics with the bear. You might say the following poem as you make the teddy bear move:

'Teddy bear, teddy bear, turn around.
(Turn teddy bear around.)
Teddy bear, teddy bear, touch the ground.
(Make teddy fall down.)'

✿ When you know that your baby is watching the teddy, move it to the side so that her eyes and hopefully her body follow it.

✿ Repeat the poem, moving the teddy bear each time. If your baby tires of this game, try it again on another day.

Where's the toy?

WHAT RESEARCH SAYS

The experiences that fill a baby's first months of life have a definitive impact on the architecture of the brain and future brain capacity.

By moving toys in and out of your baby's sight you will stimulate his curiosity, which is important for learning.

✿ Hold a favourite toy in front of your baby and then put it out of sight.

✿ Encourage him to look for the toy. Ask questions like, 'Is it in the sky?' then look up to the sky.

✿ Ask, 'Is it on the ground?' then look down to the ground.

✿ Ask, 'Is it in my hands? Yes, here it is!'

✿ As your baby develops, he will begin to look for the toy when you remove it from his sight.

✿ Once he has started to pay attention to where the toy went, he will follow your movements as you put it out of sight.

Let's bounce

WHAT RESEARCH SAYS

Bouncing and rocking are prerequisites for crawling and, later, walking.

Bouncing games are such fun for babies and they play an important part in helping little ones learn to balance.

❀ You can bounce your baby in many ways – sitting on your lap, lying with her tummy on your knees, lying with her back on your knees and rocking side to side.

❀ The following is a traditional bouncing rhyme to try:

'To market, to market, to buy a fat pig,
Home again, home again, jiggity jig,
To market, to market, to buy a plum bun,
Home again, home again, market is done.'

Note: Always support your baby securely when bouncing her.

Leg game

WHAT RESEARCH SAYS

Exercise strengthens muscles to
prepare babies for walking.

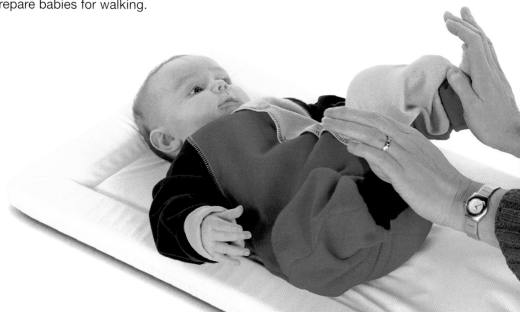

**Singing a tune as you
do this exercise will
capture your baby's
attention and develop
her language at the
same time.**

❁ Lay your baby on her back on a firm surface.

❁ Holding her ankles, bend and straighten her
legs to the following rhyme:
'One, two, three,
Bend your knees.
One, two, three,
Bend your knees.'

❁ Sing the words above to a familiar tune, or
make up your own tune.

6 to 9 months

Sing and say

WHAT RESEARCH SAYS

The earlier music is introduced, the more potential a child has for learning. Children surrounded by words almost always become fluent by three years old. Children deprived of language experiences may struggle to master speech.

Researchers at the University of Konstanz in Germany found that 'exposure to music rewires neural circuits in the brain'.

❀ Think of some of your favourite songs and sing them to your baby.

❀ Whatever songs you sing, your baby is going to enjoy hearing the words. It doesn't matter that she doesn't understand them.

❀ If your song has a familiar word that you know your little one does recognize, sing that word louder than the others.

❀ Instead of singing, try saying the same words in different ways – whispered, soft, loud and high-pitched.

❀ Whether you sing or speak the words, the rhythm will open windows of opportunity in your child's brain.

Peas and carrots

WHAT RESEARCH SAYS

Practice in hand–eye coordination will develop 'wiring' in the brain.

Babies enjoy eating with their fingers. In fact, it's an important step in developing small motor skills.

When babies can pick up food and put it in their mouths, this gives them a sense of power and control that makes them feel wonderful.

❀ Put some cooked peas and carrots on the table in front of your baby.

❀ Sing her the following song, to the tune of 'Frère Jacques':
   'Peas and carrots, peas and carrots,
   Here they are, here they are.
   Put them in your mouth, put them in your mouth.
   Yum, yum, yum,
   Yum, yum, yum.'

❀ Guide her fingers to the peas and carrots and then to her mouth. She'll probably want to feed you too.

Mirror games

WHAT RESEARCH SAYS

Since the neurons for vision begin to form very early, babies need stimulating visual experiences.

Looking into a mirror is great fun and gives your baby another perspective on who she is.

It seems that the more a baby sees, the more she wants to see.

❀ Here are some things that you can do with your baby as you look into a mirror:
- Smile.
- Shake different parts of your body.
- Make faces with silly sounds.
- Make sounds with your lips.
- Make animal sounds.
- Rock back and forth.

Where's the ball?

WHAT RESEARCH SAYS

A study at the University of Alabama found that blocks, beads, peekaboo and other 'old-fashioned' toys and games strengthened cognitive, motor and language development.

This game enhances your baby's concentration and attention skills.

❁ Sit on the floor with your baby.

❁ Hold a favourite toy in your hand and talk about it.

❁ Put the toy out of your baby's sight – behind your back, in your pocket and so on.

❁ Ask the baby, 'Where's the toy?'

❁ Take out the toy and say 'Peekaboo'.

❁ Continue playing the game and change the location of the toy each time.

Puppet peekaboo

WHAT RESEARCH SAYS

With every game of peekaboo, thousands of connections among brain cells are formed or strengthened, adding a bit more development to the complex 'wiring' that will remain largely in place for the rest of your child's life. These connections are more difficult to make later on.

Children love watching and playing with puppets.

- ✿ Put a puppet on your hand and hold it behind your back.

- ✿ Bring out the puppet and say, 'Peekaboo, *(child's name)*'.

- ✿ Now put it behind your back again.

- ✿ Continue doing this until your baby begins to anticipate the puppet coming out.

- ✿ Then bring the puppet out at a different place – over your head, over the baby's head. Always bring it down in front of your baby's face (not too close) when you say the peekaboo words.

- ✿ Give the puppet to your baby and see if he will imitate you.

Whoops

WHAT RESEARCH SAYS

Peekaboo games teach babies that objects that disappear will come back again. A strong, secure connection with your child will help him withstand the ordinary stresses of daily life.

Any form of peekaboo is a great favourite with young children.

✿ Sit your baby on the floor.

✿ Take a towel and put it over your face.

✿ Say the word 'peekaboo' as you take the towel off and show your face to your baby.

✿ This game usually results in gales of laughter and the more you play it, the funnier it becomes.

✿ Try putting the towel on your baby's head and see if he will pull it off.

✿ Remember to say, 'Peekaboo' each time you take off the towel.

Sounds everywhere

WHAT RESEARCH SAYS

Babies' hearts beat faster when their parents make eye contact and speak in a melodious voice.

Improving your child's listening skills will ultimately help her with language later on.

✿ Expose your baby to a variety of sounds.

✿ Crunch different kinds of paper. Cellophane and tissue paper have interesting sounds.

✿ Make sounds with your mouth and put your baby's fingers on your mouth as you make them. Here are some ideas for sounds to make:
  • Buzz like a bee.
  • Hum.
  • Pop your cheeks.
  • Make a siren sound.
  • Cough.
  • Pretend to sneeze.

Touching textures

WHAT RESEARCH SAYS

Through interaction, babies develop the network of brain cells that helps them learn to calm themselves.

Games that encourage hand–eye coordination are important to play with your baby because they help develop the wiring in her brain.

✿ Gather together objects made of different kinds of materials – wool, cotton, velvet, satin and any others that you might have.

✿ Sit on the floor with your baby and hold out one of the objects close enough for her to reach. When she grabs at it, praise her.

✿ Once she has touched the object, tell her the name of it and place it on her palm. Describe the feel of the material. For example, 'This is velvet and it feels smooth.'

✿ She will not understand all of your words, but she will associate the sound of your voice with the feel of the material.

Little stuff

WHAT RESEARCH SAYS

Small and large motor skills develop separately. Even though they require the same physical foundations, the two skills advance a little bit at a time.

You can enhance your baby's small motor skills by doing activities with her.

❀ Give your baby a variety of safe objects to play with. Start with measuring spoons, small balls and small toys.

❀ Put an object in her hand and encourage her to drop it.

❀ Give her a container to drop her treasures into and then watch her take them out.

❀ Encourage her to give you an object and then be sure to give it back.

❀ See if she can hold two things in the same hand (this might be a little hard).

One, two

WHAT RESEARCH SAYS

Babies need touching experiences to 'grow' the brain and the body. They are as critical as nutrients and vitamins.

Your baby will enjoy responding to your touch and your voice.

✿ Make up rhymes as you hold your baby's hand and let her touch different parts of your body.

✿ Here are some ideas:
  'One, two, touch my shoe.
  Yellow, red, touch my head.
  Dippity dips, touch my lips.
  Apples, pear, touch my hair.'

✿ Each time you say the body part, put your child's hand on that part. When you say, 'One, two, touch my shoe', put her hand on your shoe.

✿ Reverse the game and touch your baby as you say the rhyme.

The big squeeze

WHAT RESEARCH SAYS

Exercising small muscles has a positive effect on the motor areas of the brain.

Your baby is developing her small motor skills when she squeezes things.

Squeeze toys are great fun to play with. The rubbery kind seem to be the easiest to squeeze.

❀ If she is having trouble, put your hands over hers and squeeze the toy. Once she gets the feeling in her hands, she will be able to do it herself.

❀ Here is a fun little poem to say as you squeeze the toy:
   'Squeeze the cheese, Louise, please!
   Squeeze the cheese, Louise, please!
   Not the bees and not the trees,
   Squeeze the cheese, Louise, please!'

Waving

WHAT RESEARCH SAYS

Scientists say that creating an attachment to your baby is the most critical factor in his development. Babies will learn faster and feel better about themselves.

There are lots of opportunities to practise waving. Soon your child will be able to do this without your help.

✿ Wave your baby's feet and hands to people or pets he knows.

✿ It's best to play the game when the actual people are in the room.

✿ Sing this song, to the tune of 'Frère Jacques':
'Wave to Daddy, wave to Daddy,
Wave, wave, wave,
Wave, wave, wave.
Say hello to Daddy, say hello to Daddy,
Wave, wave, wave,
Wave, wave, wave.'

✿ You can wave with either hands or feet to Mummy, Grandma, Grandpa, friends and pets.

A pop game

WHAT RESEARCH SAYS

Holding and stroking a baby will stimulate her brain to release important hormones that allow her to grow.

Movement and music together stimulate both sides of the brain.

✿ Hold your baby in your arms as you move around the room and sing this song, to the tune of 'Pop Goes the Weasel':
> 'All around the mulberry bush,
> The monkey chased the weasel,
> The monkey thought 'twas all good fun,
> Pop! goes the baby.
> (Or say your child's name.)'

✿ When you come to the word 'pop', hold your baby high into the air, then bring her down for a kiss.

Let's climb

WHAT RESEARCH SAYS

Each young brain forms, at its own pace, the neural and muscular connections required for crawling and climbing.

There is no avoiding it! Your baby will soon begin to climb everything in sight. Why not help her along and develop her large motor muscles?

❀ Take cushions and pillows and pile them on the floor.

❀ Put your baby in front of the pillows and she will have a wonderful time.

❀ Take a favourite toy and put it on top of one of the pillows. This will entice her even more.

Love those keys!

WHAT RESEARCH SAYS

Exercising small muscles
stimulates brain development.

This is an excellent game for developing small motor skills.

Keys are a favourite toy for babies. They make a noise and are easy to hold, and babies like to drop them.

✿ Hold the keys in your hand and say, 'One, two, three, let's drop the keys.'

✿ Drop the keys on the floor and be sure your baby watches them drop.

✿ Put the keys in his hand and repeat.

✿ Open his fingers and let the keys drop.

✿ After a few times, he will know what to do and will delight in this game.

Sing about the day

WHAT RESEARCH SAYS

Songs introduce babies to speech patterns and sensory motor skills.

The more words your baby hears, the more the language sections of his brain will develop.

These musical 'conversations' will give your baby a basis for learning.

❀ Review your day in song. Make up any tune and sing about what you did that day.

❀ Sing about waking up, getting dressed, eating breakfast, driving in the car and so on.

❀ You can also sing about people in your baby's life:
  • Sing about grandparents – 'Grandma loves you and gives you a kiss.'
  • Sing about brothers and sisters – 'Sister Sue loves you, you, you.'
  • Sing about pets.

Where is the sound?

WHAT RESEARCH SAYS

Musical experiences enhance the future ability to reason abstractly, particularly in the spatial domains.

Playing games to heighten your baby's hearing awareness will help wire his brain. Such awareness is something that comes with age and experience.

❧ Take a wind-up musical toy and put it out of your baby's sight.

❧ Wind it up and ask him, 'Where's the music?'

❧ When he turns to the sound, praise him generously.

❧ Repeat this game in different parts of the room.

❧ If your baby is crawling, you can hide the music under a pillow or somewhere else so that he can crawl to it.

Baby, baby – a peekaboo game

WHAT RESEARCH SAYS

Talking to children from an early age will help them learn to speak.

Here's a rhyme that brings together all the brain games that we've played so far.

✿ Say the following rhyme and do the actions:

'Baby, baby, rock in the cradle.
(Rock your baby.)
Baby, baby, jump in the bed.
(Put your baby down on her back.)
Baby, baby, smile at your daddy.
(Hold your face close to your baby's face and smile.)
Baby, baby, wiggle your head.
(Hold your baby's head and gently move it from side to side.)
Baby, baby, play hide and seek.
(Put your hands over your eyes.)
Baby, baby, shall we peek?
(Take your hands away from your eyes.)
Baby, baby, what do you see?
(Bring your face close to your baby's face.)
I am back, yes, sireeeee!
(Give your baby a nice hug.)'

by Jackie Silberg

9 to12 months

Father, Mother and Uncle John

WHAT RESEARCH SAYS

A strong emotional bond actually affects the baby's biological systems that adapt to stress.

Try this game where you pretend to let your baby fall. Her confidence in you will outweigh any fear and she will love the sensation.

✿ Put your baby on your lap facing you and recite the following rhyme as you bounce your knees:

'Father, Mother and Uncle John
Rode to the doctor one by one,
Father fell off,
Mother fell off,
But Uncle John rode on and on.
Father fell off,
Mother fell off,
But Uncle John rode on.'

✿ On the words 'Father fell off', hold your baby tightly and pretend to fall to one side.

✿ On the words 'Mother fell off', holding your baby tightly, pretend to fall to the other side.

In and out

WHAT RESEARCH SAYS

Early experiences shape the way circuits are made in the brain.

Understanding spatial concepts like *in*, *out*, *behind*, *under* and *over* is important for brain development.

Playing games that encourage an understanding of space will benefit your baby in future years. Start with inside and outside.

✿ Take a large paper bag or a box and put a favourite toy inside.

✿ Help your baby find the toy and take it out.

✿ Put it back in again and keep playing the game over and over.

✿ Make up a silly song, such as the one below, and say it each time you put the toy back:
    'Boxy, woxy, toysie, woysie,
    Boom, boom, boom.
    (Say the last boom in a bigger voice.)'

I touch

WHAT RESEARCH SAYS

Touching babies helps their digestion and relieves stress.

This rhyme helps your baby identify her body parts.

✿ First say the following rhyme and point to each part of your body:
'I'll touch my chin, my cheek, my chair,
I'll touch my head, my heels, my hair,
I'll touch my knees, my neck, my nose,
Then I'll bend and touch my toes.'

✿ Next, take your baby's hand and point to each part of her body as you say the rhyme again, changing 'my' to 'your'.

✿ You are also saying words that begin with the same sound.

A stacking toy

WHAT RESEARCH SAYS

Helping a baby's brain 'grow' means immersing her in environments that are emotionally and intellectually rich and stimulating.

Stacking toys have lots of possibilities for developmental play.

All toys have great creative possibilities. Help your baby see the different ways to play with toys.

❀ Depending on your baby's developmental needs and skills, encourage her to try any of the following:

- Stacking large to small, small to large and any other way.
- Throwing the rings.
- Putting the rings on her fingers.
- Putting the rings in her mouth.
- Spinning the rings.

Where's the baby?

WHAT RESEARCH SAYS

Researchers now confirm that how you interact with your baby and the experiences you provide have an impact on her emotional development and learning abilities.

You can also play this game with pictures of family members and friends.

✿ Find several pictures of a baby and hide them in different places.

✿ Choose places that are familiar to your baby – on the ceiling above the changing place, in the toy box or under a plate on the highchair.

✿ Say, 'Let's find the baby.'

✿ Ask different questions: 'Is it in the sink?', 'Is it on the chair?'

✿ Finally ask the question, 'Is it in the toy box *(or other place)*?'

✿ When your baby finds the picture, praise her and clap your hands.

Jack-in-the-box

WHAT RESEARCH SAYS

Blocks, art and pretending all help children develop curiosity, language, problem-solving skills and mathematical ability.

This popular game helps reinforce the idea that surprises can be fun.

✿ Make a fist with both hands and tuck your thumb under the fingers.

✿ On the words 'Yes, I will', pop up your thumbs.
  'Jack-in-the-box sits so still.
  Won't you come out?
  Yes, I will.'

✿ Help your child make a fist and show her how to pop up her thumb.

✿ You can also play this game by crouching down and jumping up.

Bath time hickory

WHAT RESEARCH SAYS

Language skills and future language capacity develop best in an environment rich in spoken language.

'Hickory, Dickory, Dock' is a wonderful nursery rhyme to sing and play when giving your baby a bath.

'Hickory, Dickory, Dock,
The mouse ran up the clock.
The clock struck one,
The mouse ran down,
Hickory, Dickory, Dock.'

✿ Take the soap or the flannel and slowly move up your baby's arm as you sing, 'The mouse ran up the clock.'

✿ On the words 'The mouse ran down', slide the flannel down your baby's arm and make a splash in the water.

✿ You can also play this game by moving a toy up and down the side of the bath.

A twinkle game

WHAT RESEARCH SAYS

Research confirms that the highest level of music aptitude occurs immediately after birth. Infants possess an abundance of genes and synapses that immediately make them ready for learning music.

Music organizes the rhythm of language.

✿ Sit your baby on the floor facing you.

✿ Sing the song 'Twinkle, Twinkle, Little Star' while you are holding your baby's hands.

✿ On the last word of each line, clap his hands together as you emphasize the word a little louder than the others.

'Twinkle, twinkle, little STAR *(clap hands)*,
How I wonder what you ARE!
(clap hands).
Up above the earth so HIGH *(clap hands)*,
Like a diamond in the SKY *(clap hands)*.
Twinkle, twinkle, little STAR *(clap hands)*,
How I wonder what you ARE
(clap hands).'

The teeth rhyme

WHAT RESEARCH SAYS

Love is a powerful connection for a child. The expressions of that love will affect the way her brain makes connections.

This is one of those games that babies love and may use to show off to your friends and relations.

✿ Teach your baby to open her mouth and show her teeth.

✿ Stick out your tongue and see if your baby copies you.

✿ Now rub your tongue against your upper teeth.

✿ Say the following rhyme and do the actions:
  'Four and twenty white horses *(point to your teeth)*,
  Standing in a stall.
  Out came a red bull *(stick out your tongue)*,
  And licked them all (*lick your upper teeth with your tongue).*'

✿ Say it again and point to your baby's teeth and tongue.

✿ Encourage her to stick out her tongue and lick her upper teeth.

Discovering books

WHAT RESEARCH SAYS

The language journey starts in the womb, where the foetus constantly hears the sounds of her mother's voice.

Reading aloud is a wonderful gift that you can give your child.

Babies are interested in the shape of a book, pictures, turning the pages, and holding and touching a book.

✿ Point to a picture and say what it is. When you point to the same picture several times, your child will learn the name of the object or person.

✿ Ask your child, 'Where is the _____?' See if she will point to the picture.

✿ Let your baby hold, drop and turn the pages of a book. This kind of experimentation sets the path for good speech, reading and special times for you and your child.

✿ Read the same book over and over again.

Mouth songs

WHAT RESEARCH SAYS

Songs, movement and musical games of childhood are neurological exercises that help children learn speech patterns and motor skills.

As your baby is developing her language skills, she will enjoy discovering all the many things that she can do with her mouth.

✿ Pick a song that your little one enjoys hearing. Some popular ones are 'Twinkle, Twinkle, Little Star', 'Incey, Wincey Spider' and 'This Old Man'.

✿ Sing the song in different ways. Sing it in a high voice, a whispering voice, a humming voice and so on.

✿ The more ways your baby hears this song, the more she will try to copy you and develop her language skills.

Happy face

WHAT RESEARCH SAYS

Researchers have found that children are better at recalling stories that arouse strong feelings in them.

Encourage your baby to express his feelings through stories.

✿ Find pictures in magazines of children laughing and smiling. Coloured pictures are the best.

✿ Mount these pictures on cardboard and look at them with your baby.

✿ Talk about the feelings portrayed in the pictures. A happy face will become cemented in your baby's mind and will make new connections in his brain.

✿ Look at the happy face pictures with your baby and sing a song (any song!) while smiling.

Say it again

WHAT RESEARCH SAYS

Talking to babies encourages the development of a good vocabulary in the future.

Imitation is a natural skill that babies have.

✿ Say a word and encourage your baby to copy you.

✿ Pick words that she is familiar with and start with one syllable.

✿ You've probably already done this by teaching your baby, 'What does the cow say?'

✿ Each time she repeats what you say, praise her and give her a hug.

✿ Some easy words are 'light' and 'cat'. Some simple two-syllable words are 'baby', 'Daddy', 'Mummy', 'apple' and 'bye-bye'.

12 to 15 months

Song-patting

WHAT RESEARCH SAYS

For a young child's brain to grow and thrive, the child needs to be loved, held, talked to, read to and allowed to explore.

This game helps develop a child's sense of rhythm and her listening skills.

Try song-patting when changing your toddler's nappy, giving her a bath or at any time.

✿ Sing your favourite song to your toddler and, at the same time, pat her tummy, stroke her cheek or rub her back with your index finger to the rhythm of the song.

✿ Always end the song with a snuggly kiss.

✿ You can also sing one line of the song and pat only one word. For example, 'Twinkle, twinkle, little *(pat the word "star" but don't sing it)*'.

Bouncing, bouncing

WHAT RESEARCH SAYS

Positive interactions with caring adults stimulate a child's brain, causing synapses to grow and existing connections to be strengthened.

This enjoyable bouncing game is a great bonding experience for you and your toddler.

❀ Put your child on your lap. Hold him firmly under the arms.

❀ Say the following as you bounce your child:
'Bouncing, bouncing, let's go bouncing.
Up and down,
All around.
Bouncing, bouncing, let's go bouncing.
Whoops, don't fall down.
(*Tip your toddler to one side.*)'

❀ Say the poem again and 'tip' to the other side.

❀ Repeat the poem and on the word 'whoops' open up your knees while holding your toddler at the waist and let him fall back.

Yum, yum

WHAT RESEARCH SAYS

Tone and facial expressions are understood before words. Emotional learning is intertwined with all domains of learning.

Expressing pleasant emotions with your toddler is good for brain development.

✿ Develop your toddler's language skills when you prepare a meal or snack by chanting the following verse or singing it to the tune of 'The Farmer in the Dell':

'It's time to find the milk,
It's time to find the milk,
Hi, ho, the derry oh,
It's time to find the milk.'

✿ Walk to the refrigerator and take out the milk carton. Say, 'I love milk. Yum, yum.'

✿ Use the chant with other foods or household items. Take out the item, chant the verse, then talk about the food.

✿ Games like this develop language skills.

Peekaboo

WHAT RESEARCH SAYS

With every game of peekaboo, thousands of connections among brain cells are formed or strengthened, adding a bit more definition and complexity to the intricate circuitry that will remain largely in place for the rest of your child's life.

Not only is peekaboo fun for your toddler, it is also very important for 'growing' the brain.

✿ You can play peekaboo by:
- Covering your eyes with your hands.
- Putting a towel over your face.
- Hiding behind a door or large piece of furniture and popping out.
- Putting your toddler's hands over her eyes and then taking them away.
- Placing a toy or stuffed animal under a cover and pulling the cover away.
- Drawing a face on your thumb with a marker pen and hiding your thumb under the other fingers.

Practising 'parentese'

WHAT RESEARCH SAYS

Because young children pay close attention to the high-pitched, singsong speech known as 'parentese', they will learn the importance of words.

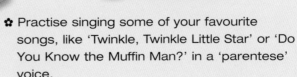

The word 'parentese' means to speak and sing to your child in a high-pitched voice.

❀ Practise singing some of your favourite songs, like 'Twinkle, Twinkle Little Star' or 'Do You Know the Muffin Man?' in a 'parentese' voice.

❀ Hold your child close to you and sing the songs two ways – first, the normal way and second, the 'parentese' way.

❀ Your toddler will pay particular attention to the second time you sing.

Lots of TLC

WHAT RESEARCH SAYS

According to Dr Bruce Perry, a psychiatrist at Baylor College of Medicine in Texas, children who don't get their quota of TLC early in life may lack the proper wiring to form close relationships.

This game develops nurturing skills.

✿ Sit on the floor with your toddler and put two or three of her favourite dolls or stuffed animals on the floor with you.

✿ Pick up one of the stuffed toys and cuddle it in your arms. Say loving words like, 'Playing with you is so much fun', 'I love your brown fur' or 'I love to hug you.'

✿ Now do the same thing to your child.

✿ Give her one of the animals and ask her to cuddle it and give it kisses.

✿ Keep the game going for as long as your toddler is interested. You will soon notice that she starts playing the game by herself.

Rock-a-bye baby

WHAT RESEARCH SAYS

Recent studies have shown how exposure to music affects spatial-temporal reasoning – the ability to see a disassembled picture and mentally piece it back together. Such reasoning underpins maths, engineering and other disciplines.

Hold your child in your arms and rock her back and forth as you sing lullabies and other soothing songs.

✿ Here are some suggestions of songs to sing:
  - 'Goodnight, Irene'.
  - 'Hush Little Baby' (The Mockingbird Song).
  - 'Kumbaya'.
  - 'Rock-a-bye Baby'.
  - 'Swing Low, Sweet Chariot'.

✿ Use a rocking motion to calm your child and develop trust between the two of you.

✿ After the last line of the song, hold your toddler close and give her a big hug.

Reading games

WHAT RESEARCH SAYS

Reading or telling a story to your child will help 'grow' her brain and encourage her to associate books with what she loves the most – your voice and closeness.

There are many ways you can help your toddler develop a love of reading.

✿ Encourage your toddler to play with touch-and-feel books and books made from cloth or sturdy cardboard.

✿ Point to pictures in books and name the various objects.

✿ Sing the nursery rhymes in books.

✿ Vary the tone of your voice, make funny faces or do other special effects when you read, to stimulate your child's interest.

✿ Read to your toddler often, but for short periods of time.

Crawl to the toy

WHAT RESEARCH SAYS

Minerals in the body are the raw materials necessary for building brain connections. One reason some children learn to crawl and walk earlier than others is that they produce minerals earlier in their development.

It's a lot of fun to crawl around in a circle with your child.

When your toddler is crawling, encourage this movement with the following game.

✿ Place a favourite toy at one end of the room.

✿ Get down on the floor and crawl to the toy. When you reach the toy, pick it up and pretend that it says, 'Come on, *(child's name)*, can you come and get me?'

✿ Encourage your little one to crawl to the toy.

✿ If your child is getting ready to walk, place the toy at a higher level so that she will try to pull herself up to reach it.

The pushing game

WHAT RESEARCH SAYS

If the brain's neurons that are connected with sight and motor skills are not trained at an early age, by adulthood they will simply not be 'plastic' enough to be rewired for many experiences.

Pushing games make a young child feel powerful and in control. They are a wonderful way to develop a toddler's confidence and coordination.

✿ Select several items for your child to push. Choose very lightweight objects such as a stuffed animal, a small toy or a push toy.

✿ Say, 'One, two, three, push', and then push one of the toys.

✿ Repeat the counting and encourage your child to do the pushing.

✿ When your little one keeps saying 'tree' (meaning the word 'three') all day long, you will know that she loves this game!

15 to 18 months

Sing out

WHAT RESEARCH SAYS

The earlier a child is introduced to music, the more potential she has for learning and enjoying music.

Develop your child's musical abilities and sensibilities by singing to her.

Don't worry about singing in key or changing the words of a song. Enjoying the singing is the important part.

✿ The following are suggestions for songs, although any song you know and love would be fine:
  - 'If You're Happy and You Know It'.
  - 'I'm a Little Teapot'.
  - 'Going to the Zoo'.
  - 'Five Little Ducks'.
  - 'Incey, Wincey Spider'.
  - 'This Old Man'.
  - 'Skip to My Lou'.

✿ Sing the song again and add actions.

✿ Move your toddler's hands for clapping, waving and so on. Do the action first and then let your toddler do it.

✿ Enjoy singing with your toddler any time during the day – while you are in the car, waiting in the queue at the supermarket or sitting in a doctor's waiting room. Any time is a good time to sing.

Playing with texture

WHAT RESEARCH SAYS

Children who grow up in an environment rich in language are almost always fluent by the age of three. People deprived of language as children struggle to master it, no matter how smart they are or how intensively they're trained.

This game develops tactile awareness and language skills.

✿ Put together several objects with interesting textures for your toddler to experience, such as something hard (a block) and something soft (a squishy toy).

✿ Put her hand on a hard item you have chosen and say the name of the item with the word 'hard' before it. For example, 'Hard block.' Now put her hand on something else that is hard and say the name again. For example, 'Hard table.'

✿ Do this several times and then introduce the soft items, such as a soft rug or a soft pillow.

✿ When you say the word 'hard' use a hard-sounding voice, and when you say the word 'soft' use a soft voice.

Everything can talk

WHAT RESEARCH SAYS

Speak slowly and with careful enunciation so the young child can distinguish individual words. Emphasizing or repeating one word also helps.

This is a playful way to develop a child's language skills.

✿ Take a favourite stuffed animal, such as a teddy bear, and hold it up to your ear as if you are listening to what it is saying. Tell your toddler that teddy says, 'Let's play.'

✿ Use a high-pitched voice when you say the words, 'Let's play.'

✿ Give the teddy to your toddler and ask him what he thinks teddy said.

✿ Continue playing the game by asking what different toys or objects in the room say. For example, a chair can say, 'Soft.'

✿ Always use a high-pitched voice when speaking for the toy or object.

Rolling fun

WHAT RESEARCH SAYS

Every new move has to be repeated over and over to strengthen neural circuits that wind from the brain's thinking areas into the motor cortex and out to nerves connected to muscles.

You can develop your child's motor skills by rolling a ball to her and encouraging her to roll it back.

Your toddler has reached the age where rolling balls is fun to do. Try the following.

✿ Sit on the floor with your child. Call out her name so she will look at you, then roll the ball to her.

✿ Encourage her to roll it back to you.

✿ As you are rolling, chant the words, 'I roll the ball to *(child's name)*.'

✿ When she rolls the ball back to you chant, '*(Child's name)* rolls the ball to *(Daddy)*.'

✿ Only chant the words when the actual rolling is taking place.

Early block fun

WHAT RESEARCH SAYS

Small and large motor skills develop independently, although they require the same physical foundations. If a child is putting lots of effort into large motor skills one week, he won't be working much on small motor skills at the same time.

Stacking blocks help develop small motor skills.

❀ You can play this with bought building blocks but it is more fun to make your own.

❀ Make disposable blocks out of small milk cartons. Tape the ends together and cover the cartons with sticky-backed paper.

❀ Encourage your toddler to decorate the blocks with crayons or stickers.

❀ Play a stacking game, praising him each time he stacks one block on top of another.

❀ Sometimes he will have more fun knocking down the stacks.

Story time

WHAT RESEARCH SAYS

Reading books aloud to children stimulates their imagination and expands their knowledge of the world. It helps them develop language and listening skills and prepares them to understand the written word.

This game develops a toddler's pre-reading skills and encourages her to love books and reading.

When reading to your child be aware of the following.

❀ Reading books to toddlers can be frustrating. It's important to realize that two to four minutes is about as long as they can sit still.

❀ Toddlers are interested in books with photos of children doing familiar things like eating, running and sleeping.

❀ Books about saying hello and goodbye are popular with children of this age.

❀ Simple rhymes and predictable text are also important criteria.

❀ To increase your child's interest in a book, substitute her name for the name of a child in the book.

❀ You can read anywhere – on a bed, at bath time (using waterproof books, of course!), sitting on the floor or in a swing.

The cuddle game

WHAT RESEARCH SAYS

Young children fall in love with their parents. Psychologists call it 'attachment'. First postulated by British psychiatrist John Bowlby in the 1950s, attachment remains one of this century's more enduring theories of human development.

Cuddling your toddler is a very important way to build his brain capacity.

In times of danger, cuddling is even more important. It also engenders the development of trust.

✿ If your little one wanders where he is not allowed to go, pick him up and cuddle him while explaining, 'You cannot go there because it is dangerous.'

✿ He will understand by the tone of your voice that what he did is a 'no-no'.

✿ By the way that you hold him as you say those words, he will also understand that you care and want to protect him.

Going to the park

WHAT RESEARCH SAYS

Helping a child's brain 'grow' means immersing her in environments that are rich and stimulating, both emotionally and intellectually.

This game develops your toddler's language skills.

Toddlers love their stuffed toys, and you will often hear them carrying on a conversation with a stuffed animal.

❁ Engage your child in a pretend game of 'going to the park' with her stuffed toys.

❁ Ask questions that encourage her to talk. For example, 'What do you think teddy should wear today?', 'Is it cold outside?', 'If teddy doesn't wear shoes, what will happen to his feet?'

❁ More ideas for questions are 'Shall we take some lunch to the park?' and 'What does your monkey like to eat?'

❁ Always respond to what your child says, which will encourage her to talk even more.

❁ Language skills are also essential when a toddler is older and learning to read.

Looking at me

WHAT RESEARCH SAYS

Sensory experiences and social interactions with supportive adults will help your child to develop thinking abilities.

This game will help him become more aware of himself and his abilities.

❀ Look into a mirror with your toddler and let him watch his face as he does different things.

❀ As he watches himself in the mirror, ask him to do the following:
- Smile.
- Stick out his tongue and inspect it.
- Open and close his mouth.
- Look at his teeth.

❀ Give him something to eat and let him watch himself chew (with his mouth closed, of course!).

Toy sounds

WHAT RESEARCH SAYS

Exposure to a variety of musical stimuli and developing listening (auditory) skills in the early years are important to a child's mental growth.

Think about the toys that your toddler likes to play with and encourage him to make up sounds that the toys could make.

✿ Here are some suggestions:
- Trains – train sound.
- Cars – car sounds.
- Stuffed animals – made-up voices.
- Dolls – made-up voices.
- Blocks – the taller the tower, the higher the voice.

18 to 21 months

Words, words, words

WHAT RESEARCH SAYS

Children learn a language by hearing words over and over. That's why the earlier you start talking to children the better.

Pictures from books and magazines can be a great source of discussion.

✿ Cut out pictures of familiar things such as animals, babies and food from a magazine.

✿ Look at the pictures with your toddler and talk about each picture.

✿ For example, point to a cow and say, 'The cow is at the farm. "Moo, moo," says the cow.'

✿ Now ask your toddler what the cow says. If she doesn't respond, repeat your words again.

✿ Point to a baby and say, 'The baby is in the cradle. The baby says, "Waa, waa."' Then ask your toddler what the baby says.

✿ Talk about a picture that your child has already seen, then add a new picture.

✿ Let your child choose one of the pictures and tell you about it or make up a short, simple story about one of the pictures.

The classics

WHAT RESEARCH SAYS

When listening to classical music, children strengthen the brain circuits used for mathematics. Listening to music also enhances the inherent brain patterns that are used for complex reasoning tasks.

Classical music can be great to dance to. Select some fast and slow music.

❀ Dance to the music and encourage your toddler to join in.

❀ Music like 'The Flight of the Bumble Bee' (Rimsky-Korsakov) is good because it is fast and you can pretend to be a bee buzzing around the room.

❀ Classical music that is soft and gentle will relax your child and is excellent to play during nap time.

❀ Here are a few suggestions for classical music to use:
  • 'The Blue Danube' (Strauss) – infectious music you have to dance to.
  • 'Carnival of the Animals' (Saint-Saëns) – the instruments imitate animals.
  • 'William Tell Overture' (Rossini) – familiar, lively music.
  • 'The Nutcracker' (Tchaikovsky) – excellent for acting out.
  • 'Clair de Lune' (Debussy) – music that describes moonlight.

Tops and bottoms

WHAT RESEARCH SAYS

Teaching concepts such as *top* and *bottom* nurtures connections that develop the capacity of the brain.

As well as spatial concepts this game will help to develop small motor skills.

✿ Sit on the floor with your toddler.

✿ Take three or four blocks and build a tower.

✿ Take a toy and put it on top of the blocks and say, 'The toy is on the top.'

✿ Knock the toy off the top of the tower and say, 'The toy is on the bottom.'

✿ Repeat the game, letting your toddler move the toy from top to bottom.

Can you find me?

WHAT RESEARCH SAYS

From the moment a baby is born, each and every experience builds the neural connections that guide development.

This is a very popular game with toddlers.

❀ Pick a favourite stuffed animal.

❀ Hide the animal while your toddler is watching.

❀ Say the following:
   'Where is bunny rabbit
   (or another stuffed animal)?
   Where could he be?
   Let's find him as quick as "one, two, three".'

❀ Go to the place that the bunny has been hidden and pull it out. Say, 'Here is rabbit, hooray!'

❀ Continue the game by hiding other toys. Always say the rhyme (changing the name of the stuffed animal) before you find the toy.

❀ Ask your toddler to hide a toy. Repeat the rhyme and let him find it.

Different voices

WHAT RESEARCH SAYS

Early childhood experiences have a dramatic impact, physically determining how the intricate neural circuits of the brain are 'wired'.

Talking and singing in different voices are good ways to encourage language development.

✿ Sing a simple song that you know.

✿ First sing it in a normal singing voice.

✿ Now change your voice and try to get your toddler to do the same. Try different voices, including:
  • High voice.
  • Low voice.
  • Soft voice.
  • Nasal voice (hold your nose as you sing).

✿ This kind of game will help your young child learn about patterns of speech.

Hippety hoppity

WHAT RESEARCH SAYS

An adult's vocabulary is largely determined by speech heard within the first three years.

Children love action rhymes. If your child has a favourite toy, make up a poem of your own.

❀ Develop your toddler's language skills by saying the following poem and doing the actions:
> 'Hippety hoppity, hippety hoppity *(jump like a bunny rabbit)*,
> Hippety hoppity, stop.
> *(Stop jumping.)*
> I'm so tired, I'm so tired *(yawn)*.
> I think I'm going to flop.
> *(Fall down on the ground.)*'

  by Jackie Silberg

❀ When you have stopped hopping, ask your child why the bunny rabbit was so tired.

❀ Suggest things the rabbit might have seen while he was hopping around.

❀ Talk about the places the rabbit might have gone – into your garden, down the street or behind a bush.

❀ Give your child the words and before you know it, she will be making up her own poem.

Someone special

WHAT RESEARCH SAYS

When children have a nurturing environment early in life, they often have higher IQ scores and adjust more easily to school.

✿ Develop your toddler's listening skills by saying the following poem to him:
'I know someone very special.
Do you know who?
I'll turn around and turn around *(turn around)*,
And then I'll point to you *(point to your child)*!'

by Jackie Silberg

This game develops your child's listening skills because he must listen to know what to do.

✿ Ask him to turn around as you say the poem.

✿ Repeat the poem and change the action. Instead of turning around, jump up and down, clap your hands, fly like a bird and so on.

Cat and mouse

WHAT RESEARCH SAYS

Exercising forms and strengthens neural bridges that are necessary for learning academic skills in later life.

This game is not only great fun but also a wonderful way to develop large motor muscles.

✿ Tell your toddler that you are a tiny little mouse and that she is a cat that is going to chase you.

✿ Tell her that the mouse says, 'Squeak, squeak', and the cat says, 'Meow, meow.'

✿ Get down on the floor and say, 'You can't catch me!' Start crawling quickly and encourage your child to chase you.

✿ Crawl behind furniture, under tables and into other rooms.

✿ When your child understands the game, swap roles.

Listen to the sound

WHAT RESEARCH SAYS

Expose your toddler to a variety of sensory stimuli – colours, music, language, natural and mechanical sounds, touch, smell, taste – to ensure that, as an adult, he will have the most flexible brain power for learning.

This game will help your toddler become aware of the wonderful sounds of the outdoors.

✿ Take your toddler outside.

✿ Start listening for birds. When you hear a bird chatter or sing, try to copy the sound and tell him that you are making the 'birdie sound'.

✿ If you continue this, he will become aware of the sound and may try to duplicate it.

✿ Add new sounds, such as the wind blowing or dogs barking.

✿ Listen for other sounds in your environment, such as car sounds, motorcycle sounds and train sounds.

Animal talk

WHAT RESEARCH SAYS

By listening, watching and giving words to experiences, you demonstrate interest in children and make them feel that their thoughts and words are important.

Toddlers love to make animal sounds and this game will help them associate sounds that go with different animals.

❁ Show your toddler a picture of a dog. Talk about the sound that the dog makes.

❁ Next show her a picture of a cat and talk about the sound that the cat makes.

❁ Now show her a picture of a fish and, instead of making a sound, show her how the fish moves its mouth.

❁ Say the following:
'What does the doggie say?
"Woof, woof, woof."
What does the kitty say?
"Meow, meow, meow."
But the fishie, oh, the fishie
Goes *(move your mouth like a fish)*.'

❁ The next time, start with a familiar animal, then add a new animal and its sound. You could look at pictures before you say the poem.

❁ Always end with the fish. A familiar end will give your child a feeling of security.

21 to 24 months

Sharing music

WHAT RESEARCH SAYS

Musical experiences are vital to speech and motor development and to sensory integration.

Sharing music with your toddler will benefit his brain and give you both a lot of pleasure.

❀ Play a variety of music (any kind that you and your child enjoy listening to) and respond to your child's movements. If he sways, you sway. If he jumps, you jump.

❀ Hold his hand and do different movements to the music. You can jump, slide, run, twirl and tiptoe.

❀ Move freely to the music and let your toddler do the same. When he sees that you are enjoying the music, he will enjoy it too.

Dressing up

WHAT RESEARCH SAYS

The size of a two-year-old's vocabulary is closely linked to how much an adult talks to the child. At 20 months, children of chatty mothers had on average 131 more words than children of less talkative mothers; at two years, the gap had more than doubled to 295 words.

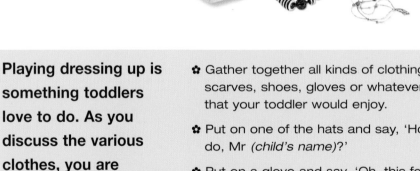

Playing dressing up is something toddlers love to do. As you discuss the various clothes, you are developing their language and giving them new vocabulary.

❀ Gather together all kinds of clothing – hats, scarves, shoes, gloves or whatever you think that your toddler would enjoy.

❀ Put on one of the hats and say, 'How do you do, Mr *(child's name)*?'

❀ Put on a glove and say, 'Oh, this feels so smooth.'

❀ Encourage your child to pick an article of clothing. Help him with words if he doesn't have his own.

❀ Soon a conversation will develop and the language will flow.

Talk to the animals

WHAT RESEARCH SAYS

Scientists have shown that in stressful situations children who have a secure attachment to a parent or carer adapt more easily and produce less cortisol, a stress hormone that affects the metabolism, the immune system and the brain.

Acting out everyday situations helps your toddler understand them.

❀ Pick a favourite stuffed animal that your child likes to play with.

❀ Carry on a conversation with the stuffed friend:
  You: 'I took your biscuit and ate it.'
  Stuffed friend: 'Thank you for telling me.'
  You: 'Can I get you another one?'
  Stuffed friend: 'Yes, thank you *(pretend to eat a biscuit)*.'
  You: 'I like to play dressing up with you.'

Stuffed friend: 'I like to wear the red scarf.'
You: 'Let's pretend it's winter.'
Stuffed friend: 'And it's snowing.'

❀ Think up situations to act out with your toddler that can teach him about important events or situations in his life.

❀ Encourage him to enter into the conversation.

❀ Other ideas for conversation are putting away toys, brushing teeth and going to the doctor.

The looking game

WHAT RESEARCH SAYS

A child's potential is determined in the early years – from the first moments of life to the age of three. These are the years when we create the promise of a child's future.

This game will require your toddler to concentrate, he needs to listen carefully to your instructions then carry them out.

✿ Place a few familiar toys on each side of the room.

✿ Sit on the floor with your toddler.

✿ Show him how to lift his chin high in the air.

✿ Show him how to turn his head to one side and then the other side.

✿ Ask him to look at (name a toy) as he turns his head in different directions.

✿ Repeat places for him to look – look at the ceiling, look at the floor and so on.

Learning with play

WHAT RESEARCH SAYS

Brain research underscores what educators have long argued: early social and emotional experiences are the seeds of human intelligence. Each child's neural circuits are carving highways in the brain where future learning will travel with ease.

This is a great game to develop your toddler's thinking skills and help him imagine other things to do with the same object, such as using a cup to drink from and for pouring.

- ✿ Select several objects, such as a hairbrush, a spoon or a cup that your toddler is familiar with and uses on a regular basis.

- ✿ Set them on the floor.

- ✿ Sit in front of the objects.

- ✿ Pick up one object, such as the hairbrush, and pretend to brush your hair.

- ✿ Pick up each object and pretend to use it.

- ✿ Ask your toddler to pick up one of the objects and show you how he would use it.

Singing names

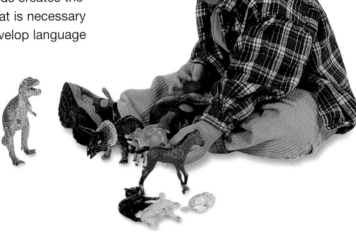

WHAT RESEARCH SAYS

The more words a child hears, the faster he learns language. The sound of words creates the neural circuitry that is necessary for children to develop language skills.

This is a great vocabulary-building game.

- ✿ Sit on the floor with your child.

- ✿ Name an object in the room that the child knows by chanting or saying, 'I can see a teddy bear' (or other familiar object).

- ✿ Ask your child to touch the teddy bear.

- ✿ Continue by naming another object in the room. Each time you name an object, chant or say it in the sentence first, then ask your child to touch the object.

Clap your hands

WHAT RESEARCH SAYS

Before a child can process language, he can process music. Early musical experiences increase and enhance spatial-temporal reasoning and the learning of mathematical concepts.

When children do fast and slow actions, they begin to internalize the concepts.

✿ Sing the following very slowly to the tune of 'Row, Row, Row Your Boat':

'Clap, clap, clap your hands,
Slowly every day.
(Clap your hands slowly.)
Merrily, merrily, merrily, merrily
(keep clapping),
Then we shout, "Hooray".
(Jump up and down and shout "hooray" slowly.)'

✿ Sing this verse faster.

'Clap, clap, clap your hands,
Faster every day.
(Clap your hands faster.)
Merrily, merrily, merrily, merrily,
Then we shout, "Hooray".'

by Jackie Silberg

✿ Sing this song with different actions. Always do the actions slowly at first, then speed them up.

✿ Other actions to try include rolling your hands, shaking your hands, waving your hands, stamping your feet and shaking your hips.

Old MacDonald

WHAT RESEARCH SAYS

A neurological scan of children who are singing nursery rhymes and doing counting games would show sections of their brains literally glowing with activity.

A favourite song with toddlers is 'Old MacDonald Had a Farm'. They love to make the animal sounds.

✿ Try singing a new version of the song:
'Old MacDonald had a cold, E, I, E, I, O. And with his cold he had a cough, E, I, E, I, O.'

✿ Add sounds you might make when you have a cold.

✿ Old MacDonald could also have a garden, a house, a sweet shop and so on. Changing the words develops vocabulary.

✿ For a challenge, sing this as a sequential song, repeating the list of items mentioned at the end of each verse.

Oh, my goodness!

WHAT RESEARCH SAYS

When children receive warm, responsive care, they are more likely to feel safe and secure and to be able to build attachments to others.

This rhyme will encourage a sense of security in your child.

❀ Say the following to your child:
  'Oh, my goodness,
  Oh, my gracious,
  Look who's here, look who's here.
  Oh, my goodness,
  Oh, my gracious,
  It's my favourite *(child's name).*'

❀ Hold your child close and give her a big hug.

❀ Repeat the poem again. When you hug your child, hold her high in the air and then bring her down for a big kiss.

❀ Try rocking her, slowly spinning her around or any other loving motion.

❀ Your little one will absolutely love this!

Rickety roo

WHAT RESEARCH SAYS

A child's brain grows through experience and attachment, two critical components necessary to a child's development.

Your child will want to do this over and over again. It's the perfect way to develop attachment skills.

❀ Put your toddler on your lap facing you. Hold her at the waist and move your knees up and down so that she can bounce.

❀ Say the following rhyme:
'Rickety roo, Rickety ree,
Bouncing on your Daddy's knee.
Rickety roo, rickety row,

Stop the horsy,
Whoooaaa.
(Pull your child close to you and give her a hug.)'

❀ Start the bouncing again, saying the following:
'Rickety roo, rickety rup,
Going up, up, up.
(Lift your child in the air.)
Rickety roo, rickety round,
Watch *(child's name)* going down!
(Support her under the arms as she falls between your knees.)'

by Jackie Silberg

24 to 27 months

Looking for faces

WHAT RESEARCH SAYS

When you express different emotions, you stimulate the brain. Emotions cause a release of chemicals that helps the brain remember different feelings and the events that are related to those feelings.

This game helps two-year-olds identify their feelings.

✿ Sit with your two-year-old and find pictures of faces in magazines and books.

✿ Ask your child about the expression on the faces.

✿ Find a picture of a child's face that looks happy. Describe the emotion on the face of the picture and then ask your child to 'make a happy face'.

✿ Keep looking for happy-face pictures.

✿ On another day look for different kinds of expressions. Excited, sad and silly are good ones.

✿ Look for expressions that match the way your child is feeling that day.

Ring-a-ring o' roses

WHAT RESEARCH SAYS

All children learn. What they learn depends on what they have been exposed to. Because most of your child's brain development takes place after birth, you have many opportunities every day to contribute to his healthy brain development.

This is a wonderful way to develop your child's spatial understanding.

✿ Play the usual 'Ring-a-ring o' Roses' with your two-year-old. Hold hands, walk around in a circle and sing the following words:
  'Ring-a-ring o' roses,
  A pocketful of posies,
  A-tishoo, a-tishoo,
  We all fall down.'

✿ Fall down to the ground gently. Your child will absolutely love this!

✿ Now play the game again, but instead of saying 'all fall down', change the action.
  'Ring-a-ring o' roses,
  A pocketful of posies,
  A-tishoo, a-tishoo,
  Turn around.'

✿ You could also clap your hands; hop, hop, hop; jump up and down; and quack like a duck.

Look at yourself

WHAT RESEARCH SAYS

Brain studies indicate that parents and educators have a golden opportunity to develop a child's brain. That means providing a rich environment without undue academic stress.

This is a wonderful game to help your child think about the different parts of his body and to enhance his observation skills.

✿ Say to your two-year-old, 'If you are wearing shoes, jump up and down.'

✿ Help your child by asking him, 'Are you wearing shoes? Show me where they are.'

✿ Point to his shoes and ask him to jump up and down. You might need to demonstrate how to do the jumping.

✿ Each time you ask him about himself, point to that part of his body and show him how to do the actions.

✿ Here are other ideas:
  • If you are wearing socks, twist back and forth.
  • If you are wearing a shirt, clap your hands.
  • If you are wearing trousers, shake your head up and down.

✿ Once you have played this game a few times, you will find that your child may be able to do the actions without your help.

Sweet little bunny

WHAT RESEARCH SAYS

Scientists have found that your relationship with your child affects her brain in many ways. By providing warm, responsive care, you strengthen the biological systems that help her handle her emotions.

This game will develop your child's spatial concepts.

✿ Play this game using your two-year-old's favourite stuffed animal. Change the name of 'bunny' to whatever stuffed animal that you are using.

✿ Say the following poem and do the actions:

'Sweet little bunny,
Hopping on the ground.
(Hold the bunny and hop it up and down.)

Sweet little bunny,
Looking all around.
(Turn the bunny around.)
Look up high.
(Hold the bunny high in the air.)
Look down low.
(Bring the bunny down to the ground.)
Run, run, run.
(Run with bunny.)
Oh, oh, oh,
Sweet little bunny,
Where did you go?
(Hide the bunny behind your back.)'

Learning rhymes

WHAT RESEARCH SAYS

Memory is learning that sticks. When learning occurs, new synapses form and/or old synapses are strengthened.

Two-year-olds are like sponges. They hear something once and are already beginning to memorize it, especially if it involves actions.

An interesting way to say nursery rhymes is to accent the last word of each line and do an action at the same time. This will help your child to memorize the rhyme.

✿ Here is an example. Remember to accent the last word:

'Hickory, dickory, DOCK.
(Move your fingers in a climbing motion.)
The mouse ran up the CLOCK.
(Climb your fingers up again.)
The clock struck ONE *(hold up one finger)*,
The mouse ran DOWN.
(Move the one finger downwards.)
Hickory, dickory, DOCK.
*(Clap your hands on the word "dock".)'

Shake your fingers

WHAT RESEARCH SAYS

Positive early experiences and interactions affect a child's emotional development.

Play this game with a doll or stuffed toy that has hands and feet.

✿ Sit on the floor with your two-year-old and show her how to take the doll's or stuffed toy's arms and shake them up and down.

✿ Give the toy to your child and let her try it.

✿ Think of all the things that you can do with the stuffed toy.

✿ Here are some ideas:
- Wave your hand.
- Clap your hands.
- Clap your feet together.
- Throw a kiss.

✿ Ask your two-year-old for her ideas.

Whispering

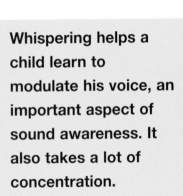

WHAT RESEARCH SAYS

Each time a child is stimulated to think, either new neural bridges are formed or pre-existing ones are strengthened. The more neural bridges formed or strengthened, the more the intellect will be developed.

Whispering helps a child learn to modulate his voice, an important aspect of sound awareness. It also takes a lot of concentration.

Two-year-olds are fascinated by whispering and are very proud when they can do it.

✿ Whisper something to your two-year-old. Say, 'Let's clap our hands.'

✿ Ask your two-year-old to whisper something back to you.

✿ Keep whispering to each other until your two-year-old understands how to make his voice very soft.

The fruit story

WHAT RESEARCH SAYS

The plasticity of the brain, its ability to rewire itself, is what makes it so easy for children to learn language. The more words young children hear, the more connections their brains make.

Everyday objects can be a great source of inspiration for conversation and language development.

❀ Pick three or four fruits for your child to examine with you.

❀ Cut each one open and talk about what's inside. Does it have seeds, a core, segments and so on?

❀ Tell a story about the fruit, using your own words. Here is an example:

'Once upon a time there was an apple that came to play with Billy. "Hi Billy, I'm glad to be here, but I am a bit lonely. Could we invite another fruit to come over and play?"

"Okay", said Billy, "I'll call an orange."

Billy dialed the phone and said, "Hello, orange. Would you like to come over to play?"'

❀ Let your child suggest whom to call next. With each new fruit, examine it, talk about it, and, of course, taste it.

Free like the wind

WHAT RESEARCH SAYS

A child's capacity to learn and thrive in a variety of settings depends on the interplay between nature (genetic endowment) and nurture (the kind of care, stimulation, and teaching they receive).

It feels wonderful to hold a scarf in your hand as you move freely to music. It also gives a child a sense of balance and control.

This is a very creative game and your child will want to play it again and again.

- ✿ Play some instrumental music as you and your child dance with scarves.

- ✿ Swoop the scarf high into the air and then low to the ground.

- ✿ Hold the scarf out as you turn in a circle.

- ✿ You and your child can each hold one end of the scarf and dance together.

- ✿ Whatever you do, your child will copy you.

27 to 30 months

Repeating

WHAT RESEARCH SAYS

Children learn language by hearing words over and over again. Language is a crucial skill since it is a primary communication system.

Play a game with your two-year-old where you repeat the last word of a sentence three times.

✿ Here are some ideas:
'Do you like ice cream, cream, cream?'
'Can I brush your hair, hair, hair?'
'Let's play with toys, toys, toys.'

✿ As you say the repeated word, accent the word the first time.

✿ Encourage your two-year-old to make up her own words and repeat them.

The mice game

WHAT RESEARCH SAYS

The number of brain connections increases when a child grows up in an enriched environment.

Fingerplays are fun ways to develop a child's language and small motor skills.

✿ Put your hands behind your back. Say the following fingerplay and do the actions:

'Five little mice went out to play *(place hands in front of you)*,
Looking for food along the way. *(Pretend to put the food in your mouth.)*
Out came the pussy cat, sleek and fat *(hold hands like claws)*,
And four little mice went scampering back.'

✿ Repeat, subtracting the number of mice that scamper back.

✿ When you get to one little mouse and you say, 'Out came the pussy cat sleek and fat', stop for a second, then say very quickly, 'The mouse ran away, now what do you think of that!'

✿ Repeat the fingerplay and encourage your child to do the actions with you.

Walkity, walkity, stop

WHAT RESEARCH SAYS

Large motor skills, small motor skills, thinking skills – everything is learned by playing. When children finally get it, their faces light up. That's what play is all about – trying different things to find out what works and what doesn't.

This game will help to develop your toddler's coordination and large muscles.

✿ Hold your child's hand as you walk and say the following:
   'Walkity, walkity, walkity, walkity,
   Walkity, walkity, stop.'

✿ Stop when you say 'stop'.

✿ Change the movement from walking to hopping.

'Hoppity, hoppity, hoppity, hoppity,
Hoppity, hoppity, stop.'

✿ Stop again when you say 'stop'.

✿ Keep changing the action, but always stop on the word 'stop'.

✿ What you will find is that your child will know the exact time to stop.

✿ Other actions you might try include jumping, swimming, turning, running and marching.

Can you do it too?

WHAT RESEARCH SAYS

At no other stage does the brain master so many activities with such ease.

This game develops your child's thinking and communication skills as well as his imagination.

✿ Pretend to use an imaginary object and tell your child what you are doing.

✿ For example, pretend to drink some milk.

✿ Say, 'I am drinking some milk.'

✿ Ask your two-year-old, 'Can you do it too?'

✿ Continue acting out simple activities that your child knows, such as the following:
  • Throw a ball.
  • Brush your teeth.
  • Wash your face.
  • Brush your hair.

✿ Always ask, 'Can you do it too?' after you do a pretend action.

The smelly game

WHAT RESEARCH SAYS

The human brain is uniquely constructed to benefit from warm, loving experiences and from good teaching, particularly during the first years of life.

Playing with fruit and flowers in this way develops your child's sensory experiences.

✿ Select three different items that have a distinct smell. It's easiest to start with food and flowers. For example, interesting smells come from an orange, a pickle and lilacs.

✿ Suggest to your child that you both pretend to be bears on a walk.

✿ Say, 'Little bear, I smell something good.'

✿ Pretend to pick an orange from a tree. Take off some of the skin and let your two-year-old smell it.

✿ Continue with the other two items that you have selected.

✿ Say, 'Little Bear, let's sit in the grass and smell these things again.'

✿ Finally, say to your little one, 'Would you like to taste one of the things that we have smelt?'

✿ When you add taste, you introduce another sensory experience.

Fill in the word

WHAT RESEARCH SAYS

Talking to children is the best way to develop their future language skills.

Two-year-olds are developing language at a very fast rate. This game is an excellent way to develop both language skills and imagination.

To encourage your two-year-old's language try the following.

❀ Make up a story with your child's name in it. Each time you come to her name, let her fill in the word.

❀ For example, 'Once upon a time there was a little girl named _____ (your child's name). This little girl named _____ (let child fill in the word) went to the kitchen to eat her lunch.'

❀ Add situations to the story that will encourage her to fill in more blanks. '_____ (Your child's name) opened the cupboard and took out some _____.'

❀ Depending on your child, you can make the story simple or complicated, short or long.

Building a house

WHAT RESEARCH SAYS

When a child is two, his brain is twice as active as that of a college student.

Make this game more exciting by giving your child plastic animals and/or people to put inside the structures he builds.

- ✿ Sit on the floor with your two-year-old and lots of building blocks.

- ✿ Make a simple structure with three or four blocks.

- ✿ If your child does not start building something on his own, encourage him to copy you.

- ✿ If your child is interested in making more complicated buildings, let him take the lead.

Looking for stones

WHAT RESEARCH SAYS

New insights into brain development affirm what many parents and carers have known for years – that loving attachments between young children and adults, and stimulation that is positive and appropriate, really do make a difference in children's development.

This enjoyable game teaches an awareness of nature.

Note: If your child still puts things into his mouth, be sure you collect only stones that do not pose a choking hazard.

- ✿ Pick a nice day to look for stones with your two-year-old.

- ✿ Talk about what you are going to do and take along a container to put the stones in.

- ✿ Suggest to your child that you look for a certain kind of stone. For example, 'Let's find a small stone' or 'Let's find a smooth stone.'

- ✿ You can look for stones that are large, small, bumpy, smooth, white, brown and so on.

- ✿ When you have finished, bring the stones home and wash them.

- ✿ Look at them closely and talk about where they might have come from.

- ✿ Let your two-year-old sort the stones.

The wheels on the bus

WHAT RESEARCH SAYS

Music optimizes brain development, enhances multiple intelligences and facilitates bonding between adult and child.

This popular song is a great favourite of young children.

✿ If you don't know the tune, you can say the words or make up your own tune.
'The wheels on the bus go round and round (*roll your fists over one another*),
Round and round, round and round (*continue rolling fists*).
The wheels on the bus go round and round,
All through the town.'

✿ Continue with other verses:
'The doors on the bus go open and shut (*use your hands*) ...
The horn on the bus goes beep, beep, beep (*pretend to honk a horn*) ...
The kids on the bus go up and down (*move up and down*) ...'

✿ And the all-time favourite verse:
'The baby on the bus goes, "waa, waa, waa" (*pretend to cry*) ...'

✿ Make up imaginative verses:
'The sheep/cows/dinosaurs on the bus go, "Baa, baa, baa" ... / "Moo, moo, moo" ... / "Grrr, grrr, grrr" ... '

My little bird

WHAT RESEARCH SAYS

Attachments between young children and their parents or carers are biologically 'wired' to forge a close emotional tie.

By holding your child close while you say this poem you will enhance your child's feeling of security.

✿ Say the following poem and do the actions:

'Here is a nest,
All warm inside,
Where my little bird
Can safely hide *(wrap your arms around your child and hold her closely)*.
Here is a nest,
All hidden away,
Where my little bird
Can sing and play *(give your child a toy)*.
Here is a nest,
All cosy and deep,
Where my little bird
Can go to sleep *(rock your little one gently and pretend to go to sleep)*.

30 to 33 months

Favourite poems

WHAT RESEARCH SAYS

Causality is a key component of logic: if I smile, Mummy smiles back. A sense that one thing causes another forms synapses that will eventually support more complex concepts of causality.

The more dramatic and fun you make this, the more your children will enjoy it. This kind of game will remain with them for ever.

Two-year-olds love the rhyme, rhythm and emotions that words conjure up, especially in poems.

❀ The following are good poems to use with young children.
  • 'Hickory, Dickory, Dock'.
  • 'Hey, Diddle, Diddle'.
  • 'Jack and Jill'.
  • 'Humpty Dumpty'.
  • 'Twinkle, Twinkle, Little Star'.
  • 'Mary Had a Little Lamb'.
  • 'Jack Be Nimble'.
  • 'Pat-a-Cake'.

❀ Say the poem with your two-year-old. Be dramatic and try acting out the story.

❀ What a fun way to learn language skills!

The sequence game

WHAT RESEARCH SAYS

During her first three years, a totally dependent child will build an incredibly complex new brain that will enable her to walk, talk, analyse, care, love, play, explore and have a unique emotional personality.

Sequencing is an important pre-reading skill. Helping your two-year-old learn to think in an orderly way will benefit her in the future.

Sequencing means doing a series of things in a certain order or pattern. It also means being able to repeat a pattern and add on to it.

✿ Self-care tasks, such as washing your hands, getting dressed or brushing your teeth, are a good place to start thinking about sequencing.

✿ Chant the following:
'Now it's time to wash our hands.
Now it's time to wash our hands.
What comes next?'

✿ Ask your child what she will do next. If she says, 'Brush my teeth', then chant that.

✿ Add the new part each time.

A treasure hunt

WHAT RESEARCH SAYS

Although the brain is capable of learning throughout life, nothing will ever again match this most exuberant time of learning.

Your child will love searching for and finding treasures.

❀ Hide three or four treasures in your garden.

❀ Tie ribbons or crêpe paper near the treasures, so that they will be easy to find.

❀ Tell your child in advance what the treasures are, such as the following:
  • Small toys hidden under some leaves.
  • Toys in a low branch of a tree.
  • Toys on the seat of a swing or at the end of a slide.

❀ Holding your two-year-old's hand, walk around the garden and search for the treasures.

Puddle watch

WHAT RESEARCH SAYS

A strong bond to a nurturing adult can help a child withstand the ordinary stress of daily life.

This kind of activity develops thinking skills. Play this game after it rains.

✿ Go outside and find a puddle.

✿ If it is on a pavement, draw a line around the puddle with chalk.

✿ If it is in a muddy area, draw a line around it with a stick.

✿ Watch it throughout the day as it dries.

✿ This brings up wonderful conversations about what has happened to the water.

Telling stories

WHAT RESEARCH SAYS

While grammar is learned more easily by hearing short sentences, children whose parents use many dependent clauses (beginning with 'because' and 'which') learn to use these in their speech earlier than the children of parents who do not.

This is a good game to play with poems.

✿ Tell a familiar story with repeated phrases.

✿ The following dialogue from 'The Three Little Pigs' is a good example of repeated phrases:
> Wolf voice: 'Little pig, little pig, let me come in.'
> Pig voice: 'Not by the hair on my chinny-chin-chin.'
> Wolf voice: 'Then I'll huff and I'll puff and I'll blow your house in.'

✿ Soon your two-year-old will be able to say the words with you.

✿ Once your child knows the words, you can begin to leave blanks and let him fill in the word.

✿ The following are additional stories, songs or folktales with repeated phrases:
- 'Goldilocks and the Three Bears'.
- 'The Three Billy Goats Gruff'.
- 'The Gingerbread Man'.

Here comes Susie Moosey

WHAT RESEARCH SAYS

Scientists are just now realizing how much experiences after birth, rather than something innate, determine the actual 'wiring' of the human brain.

✿ Say the following, using your child's name and rhyming it. For example, 'Here comes Bobby Dobby' or 'Jackie Wacky':
  'Here comes Susie Moosey,
  Walking down the street.
  She can walk a lot of ways,
  Watch her little feet.'

✿ Suggest an action for your two-year-old to do:
  'Hop Susie Moosey,
  Hop, hop, hop.
  You can hop down the street,
  With your little feet *(hop with your child)*.'

This game will develop your toddler's listening skills and coordination.

✿ Continue the game, changing the actions. Additional ideas are jump, run, tiptoe, slide, skate and march.

Sorting toys

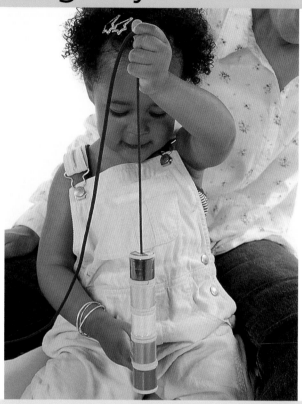

WHAT RESEARCH SAYS

Children love to play. It comes naturally to them and is something they should be encouraged to do, because it is essential to their development. Large motor skills, small motor skills, thinking skills – everything is learned through play.

This game will develop your child's thinking skills.

Two-year-olds love their toys. The more you can play games that involve their toys, the more they will enjoy it.

- ✿ Sit on the floor with your two-year-old and put many toys in front of you.

- ✿ Start sorting by colour: 'Let's find all the toys that are red and put them together.' Continue sorting by colour.

- ✿ You can sort by size, colour or characteristics (toys that have wheels, animal toys and so on).

- ✿ Ask your child how she thinks the toys should be sorted. You and she will think of many ways by looking at the toys.

When I was

WHAT RESEARCH SAYS

One thing young children need for optimum brain development is a rich and responsive language environment in which they are exposed to a wide range of vocabulary.

Develop your two-year-old's language skills and imagination by chanting about different objects in the room and making up imaginative actions for them.

✿ Chant or sing the following to the tune of 'Mary Had a Little Lamb':

'When I was a little chair,
Little chair, little chair.
When I was a little chair,
I could sit like this.

When I was a little plane,
Little plane, little plane.
When I was a little plane,
I could fly like this.

When I was a little ball,
Little ball, little ball.
When I was a little ball,
I could roll like this.'

What do you see?

WHAT RESEARCH SAYS

During critical learning periods, or windows of opportunity, pathways grow that form the foundation for future skills.

This is a very creative game that is good to play during a walk outside or a ride in the car.

✿ For example, if you are walking outside, ask your two-year-old what she sees. When she gives you an answer, stimulate her thinking by asking questions.

✿ If your child says that she sees a tree, here are some questions you could ask:

- How big is the tree?
- What colour is it?
- What do the leaves look like?
- Where is the very top of the tree and the very bottom?

Again!

WHAT RESEARCH SAYS

When the rhythm and melody of language become a part of a child's life, learning to read will be as natural as learning to walk and talk.

Reading stories will help your child have a longer attention span.

When two-year-olds like a poem, a book or a song, they want to hear it again and again.

✿ If the carer hears a story so many times that it gets boring, try asking the child to tell the story in his own words.

✿ Read the story and let your two-year-old fill in some of the words. He probably has the story memorized by now.

✿ Simple stories that your child can remember are favourites at this age.

33 to 36 months

Where is Jack?

WHAT RESEARCH SAYS

Each young brain forms the neuronal and muscular connections required for sitting and crawling, walking and talking, at its own pace.

Action songs will delight your child and as he gets to know them well he will start to join in with the words.

✿ Say the following rhyme and do the actions, then ask your two-year-old to join you:
  'I'm a little box
  (stoop down with your arms hugging your head)
  Still as can be *(stand very still).*
  Lift up my lid
  (slowly raise your hands above your head),
  And what do you see?
  Shhh! Boo!
  (Jump up and raise your hands high in the air.)
  Jack-in-the-box!'

Musical instruments

WHAT RESEARCH SAYS

Dr Mark Tramo, a neuroscientist at Harvard Medical School, reported that exposure to music rewires neural circuits. Like other circuits formed early in life, the ones for music will endure.

Provide a selection of instruments for your two-year-old to explore different kinds of sounds.

✿ Start with drums, sand blocks, triangle and sticks.

✿ Drums: hit them on the rim, then in the middle. The sound will be higher and lower.

✿ Sand blocks: rub them together to hear an interesting sound like a train.

✿ Triangle: hit it at different places to produce higher and lower sounds.

✿ Sticks: hit them on different surfaces to produce different sounds. Hitting a stick on the floor and then on a table will fascinate your child.

Let's choose

WHAT RESEARCH SAYS

The release of certain endorphins strengthens the functioning of brain connections. Positive, happy feelings cause the release of endorphins.

Play this pretend game to help your two-year-old learn about choices.

✿ Sit on the floor with your child and put several stuffed animals on the floor with you.

✿ Talk to one of the animals. 'Mr Bear, would you like cereal or cheese today?' Ask your child to answer for Mr Bear.

✿ Discuss the pros and cons of the choice.

✿ Pick up another animal and say, 'Bunny rabbit, are you going to play inside or outside today?'

✿ Here again is a good chance to discuss the answer.

✿ It is important for a child to feel good about the choices that he makes.

Muffin Man rhymes

WHAT RESEARCH SAYS

Scans of children's brains show that the growth at this age is explosive, a fact that allows them to absorb and organize new information at a rate much faster than adults.

This game helps your two-year-old learn about rhyming.

❀ Sing the tune of 'Do You Know the Muffin Man?' using the following words:

'Do you know the jo,
jo, jo,
Ho, ho, ho,
Go, go, go,
Do you know the jo, jo, jo,
Ho, ho, go, go go, hey!'

❀ As you sing the song, dance around and clap your hands on the word 'hey'.

❀ Pick any three rhyming sounds to sing the song.

Colourful steps

WHAT RESEARCH SAYS

During critical periods long, thin fibres grow inside the brain, creating pathways that carry electrical impulses from cell to cell. The resulting network, which grows daily in the young brain, forms the neurological foundation upon which a child builds a lifetime of skills.

You can develop your children's spatial thinking by expanding the actions you ask them to do.

✿ Make a trail of paper plates on the floor.

✿ Use two or three different colours in your path.

✿ Sing a favourite song as you and your two-year-old walk on the path. 'Twinkle, Twinkle, Little Star' is a good one to use.

✿ Each time you stop singing, stop walking. If your child knows colours, ask him to name the colour that you are standing on.

✿ Develop your child's spatial thinking by suggesting, 'Let's walk over the plates', 'Let's walk on the plates' or 'Let's walk around the plates.'

✿ You can also do other actions, such as hopping, jumping and tiptoeing.

The puppy game

WHAT RESEARCH SAYS

The human brain develops most rapidly from birth to the age of six. Researchers agree that personality, attitudes, concepts of self, language, coping skills and learning patterns are in place by the age of three.

Pretend play creates new opportunities for language stimulation.

✿ Designate an area of the room as the 'kennel' where the puppies play.

✿ Pretend to be the mummy or daddy dog with your two-year-old as the puppy.

✿ Ask your little puppy what his name is and call him by this name as you play the game.

✿ You can say, 'Bow wow, woof woof, (puppy's name), let's hop over to the kennel.'

✿ Follow the direction and ask your child to do the same.

✿ Continue giving ideas for different things to do in the kennel.

✿ Ask your child for his ideas.

✿ Other ideas include jumping in the kennel, marching in the kennel, crawling in the kennel and eating in the kennel. Pretend to chew on a bone, or maybe eat a real snack in the kennel.

Funny tricks

WHAT RESEARCH SAYS

If the brain's visual and motor neurons are not trained between the ages of two and eleven, by adulthood the neurons are rarely 'plastic' enough to be 'rewired'.

Sequencing games are wonderful for preparing your two-year-old for reading.

❀ Chant or sing the following to the tune of 'London Bridge is Falling Down':
  'I can do a funny trick, funny trick, funny trick,
  I can do a funny trick,
  Here's what I can do *(jump up and down).*'

❀ Repeat the song and at the end add a second activity after jumping up and down.

❀ Keep singing the song, adding on an additional activity.

❀ Additional ideas include shaking a leg, clapping hands, turning around, nodding your head and touching your toes.

Grocery shopping

WHAT RESEARCH SAYS

In the course of the first three years, a totally dependent child will build an incredibly complex brain that will be the beginning of a new independent child.

Your two-year-old will love to help you out in real-life situations.

❀ Ask your child to help you prepare a shopping list.

❀ Take her to the supermarket and look for the items on the list.

❀ When you return home, let her help you put away the groceries and read the labels, box tops and packages as you store them.

❀ If possible, make a recipe with the ingredients that you bought at the shop.

❀ Praise the efforts of your two-year-old.

A rhythm game

WHAT RESEARCH SAYS

Exposure to music rewires
neural circuits that may also
strengthen the circuits used
in mathematics.

This helps children to learn an awareness of rhythm.

✿ Say the following chant and do the actions:
'One, two, three,
Touch your knee.
One, two, three,
Knee, knee, knee.'

✿ Repeat, changing the parts of the body. For
example, 'Touch your arm' or 'Touch your
toe.'

✿ The words do not have to rhyme.

Laundry baskets

WHAT RESEARCH SAYS

Every new move has to be repeated over and over to strengthen neural circuits.

This is a great way to develop coordination.

Laundry baskets or large plastic boxes are perfect to help your child practise throwing skills.

❀ Experiment with throwing different objects, like balls, wadded paper and scarves, into the basket.

❀ Each object will require a different kind of motor skill to get it in.

❀ Place the basket close enough to your child so that he will be successful in getting the object into the basket.

Index

Acknowledgements

Acknowledgements

Executive Editor Jane McIntosh
Editor Sharon Ashman
Senior Designer Rozelle Bentheim
Designer Bill Mason

Picture Researcher Jennifer Veall
Senior Production Controller Jo Sim
All photographs Octopus Publishing
Group Ltd/ Peter Pugh-Cook